Taylor Made: A Journey of Love, Loss and Hope

Ali Taylor

BookLeaf Publishing

India | USA | UK

Taylor Made: A Journey of Love, Loss and Hope © 2024 Ali Taylor

All rights reserved.

No part of this publication may be reproduced, stored in a retrieval system, or transmitted, in any form or by any means, electronic, mechanical, photocopying, recording or otherwise, without the prior written permission of the presenters.

Ali Taylor asserts the moral right to be identified as the author of this work.

Presentation by *BookLeaf Publishing*

Web: www.bookleafpub.com

E-mail: info@bookleafpub.com

ISBN: 9789363313545

First edition 2024

For George, the way I miss you is sometimes more than I can bear, but I wouldn't trade the love we had for the pain I feel at losing you.

For my daughter, one day you will read this, and I hope you know that your sparkle and shine gave me so much strength, courage, and love. You are the greatest thing that your father and I could have ever done.

ACKNOWLEDGEMENT

I cannot thank Addie enough for her support and help in this process, from getting my words out and onto paper to getting it through publishing. And thank you to all who unknowingly became fodder for which I wrote how it felt.

You Said

You always said
I'm free to be me
To do what I please
Anything I could be
But when you saw
Just what that was
You were disappointed
And I cried because
You said, you said
"Fly away little bird
Go off, see the world
Tell the stories to be heard"
And I did and I saw
And I told them all
But I changed and
Now I'm not so small.
I've worked so hard
To find out who I am
Played the game of life
Now here I stand
But what's worst of all
What hurt the most
Are the things you say
When you should boast.
You said, you said
I'll always have you

You'd always love me
I'd never disappoint you
But you lied then
And now you say
You'll decide if
I can stay.
I've played out who
I want to be
And it kills me that
Somehow you don't see
That I'm happy now
I'm not such a little bird
I've told my story
I hope you heard.

I can't count on you

I can't count on you
I don't know what else to do
You say you will be there
But *there* turns to *nowhere*
We set a time to meet
I think it's going to be sweet
But then the time comes
And I feel like a bum
Stood up again, more the norm
Trying to calm my inner storm
But what I am learning
While I am yearning
Is that you just may not care
About the things we could share
What I find so important
Could lead to an argument
And that doesn't feel right
And I don't want to fight
It doesn't feel fair to me
To carry that burden, see
So now I know what to do
Because I can't count on you.

Tomorrow

Tomorrow has to be better
This life here isn't the one for me
I know somewhere out there
Something is greater, it's gotta be
There is so much to look forward to
Potential on the horizon
I will seize the opportunity
I am not one to frighten
I look around my world
And I feel something missing
It's like I'm stuck right here
Wanting something promising
There isn't much to look back on
Some childhood memories fond
But really, it's the future
A life that lays beyond
One day, tomorrow will come
And I will know it when it's here
So until then, I will wait
And shed a single tear.

Mine

I will walk the line
But I will take what is mine
Don't you think that's fine?

Should I be gentle
Be a demon or angel
Each has potential

Hold my hand, won't you?
Let us show them what we do
She can not redo

Her loss is my gain
I hate to cause so much pain
Cleanse the past with rain

Let time heal the wound
It will always be too soon
No one is immune

Your heart is mine now
Please exit the scene, but how
Time to take a bow.

Trust In Me

It's so hard sometimes
To simply believe
That in our world today
Not everyone is out to deceive
More often than not
It's just a game of
Get what you get
And it's not love
So close your eyes
And trust in me
I'll show you the world
That you want to see
All I need
Is to take your hand
Just come with me
And make that stand
Follow my lead
And others will too
Trust in me and
The change starts with you
Can you see the light
It's deep but grab ahold
Take the reins of life
Be daring and be bold
Hold on to the thought
If for no reason than because—

It is what it is, it ain't what it ain't
And it won't be what it never was
Don't look back, just leap
If you dare to jump
Possibilities are out there
Or hide in your slump.

This Could be Everything

This could be everything
You make my heart sing
When you hold my hand
I know you will understand
I've never felt like this before
Love is opening the door
I was sealed off and scared
But I never would have dared
To take this leap on my own
Much more than love you've shown
It's the way you look at me
It's who I want to be
It's the way you say my name
I know you feel the same
There is nothing we can't do
Together, just us two
It's you and me against the world
Into one, our lives have swirled
I could watch the sun rise and set
And nothing would make me regret
All the time we spend together
Each day, it just gets better
One day you'll give a ring
And this could be everything.

Unshining knight

Here I sit up in my tower
More alone each passing hour
Looking out and far below
I see something, but not a glow.
He is moving quickly forward
No one could call him a coward
It's as if he knew I was up here
Almost like our hearts did steer
Closer and closer he came along
And inside I broke out in a song
But I kept it in, held it close inside
Some things are just meant to hide
Finally here he is, my knight so tall
Thankfully not shining, not at all
Covered in grease and motor oil
Sweat from a hard day's toil
The smile on his face, ear to ear

To be without him is my only fear
What's mine becomes his, I share
But he doesn't seem to care
Things are things but this is more
Together we walk out the tower door
He says as long as I don't sing
He knelt down and held up a ring
A promise I was happy to make
I can't sing, for goodness sake.

Once Upon a Time

Once upon a time, we had it all
Good jobs, fun times having a ball
Living the life that we made
Basking but throwing no shade
Dual income, no kids, DINKs,
Great term, don't you think?
There was nothing else our life needed
But then one of us pleaded
That a little one was right
Now was the time, kids in sight
We set a goal and got to work
Waiting for a visit from the stork
When you take that test
Two lines are the best
And such joy explodes
To a baby leads all roads
So many thoughts develop
Until you learn it's a set-up
It isn't real, it didn't stick
The thought makes you sick
For a moment, life grew
But that time was too few
We didn't get the happy end
And I feel like I have to defend
What I didn't do wrong
Why it didn't last very long

It's not like it was my fault
I keep that thought in a vault
Pull out a happy face
Try not to take up space
Everyone wants to talk baby
So don't say it yet, maybe
But once it's gone, never comes
It feels like they only shun
There is time to try again
I think hope is what they intend
But it's not that easy to forget
The little one you'll never get.

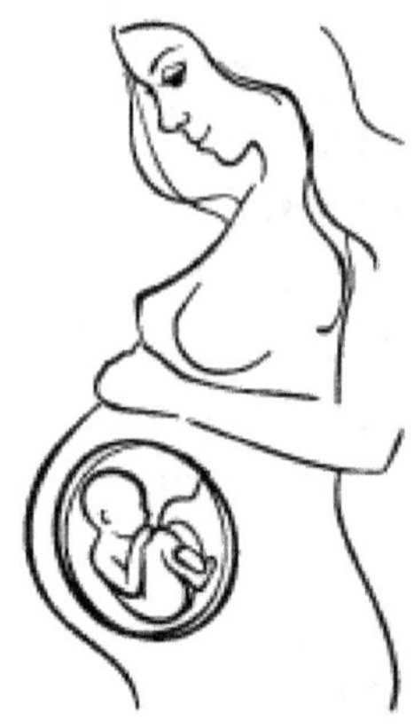

The Love of My Life

I cannot believe how lucky I am
To be searching and then—bam!
Here I find someone like you
I didn't know what to do
All my insecurities just scram

The look on your face
The nonexistent space
Between the two of us
How easy it is to trust
My heart winning the love race

It's weird how fast it all came about
From the rooftops I want to shout
Together we are so perfect
Even though you're more direct
No part of me has doubt

Oh, the way you make me feel
It seems almost unreal
I'm filled with so much love
Everything I've been in search of
All my faults you conceal

Basking in your presence
By far you are my preference

Everyone can see
All that you mean to me
Let's make them all jealous.

Sparkle

There is a sparkle in my princess
Watch her twirl and spin
See the smile in her eyes
Beaming bright from her grin
She dances there and plays here
She is so light and free
She has no idea how I need her
All that she means to me
She is building up her small world
Filling it with little joys
The things she holds closest to her
So much more than just her toys
My daughter is the best thing
That I have ever done
In a world filled with pain
All she sees is love and fun
I could snuggle her all day
Her heart is so big and pure
She is the light in the world
Of that I am sure
Don't get me wrong
She is mighty while small
A fierceness within
And she can do it all
As she dances and plays
More precious than a pearl

I give her the world
This sparkle-filled girl.

Day After Day

Day after day I have to remember
I have to tell myself to breathe
Something lies down below
But it's hidden, still sheathed

My brain doesn't function
It can't seem to move on its own
It's just like my body, frozen
Slowly turning to stone

I know something is wrong
But what, I'm not quite sure
Give me just a moment
My thoughts are on detour

Fingers, toes, arms, legs
All present and accounted
I am complete then, I guess
Not yet, my insides shouted

But what could be missing?
Take a moment, let it sink
This hole inside starts to grow
I know what it is, I think

You're gone now, aren't you?
My life, my love, my heart
The best thing about me
That's my missing part

There isn't time to stop
There is so much left to do
Calls to make, paperwork
All I want is you

I can't believe that this is real
Wake me up from this dream
Because one more breath
And I think I just might scream.

Last breath

The moment that I found you
Lying face down on the ground
I thought I saw you breathing
That I heard you make a sound
I felt your body but didn't realize
It was more that just cold
I didn't know that never again
Would I have you to hold
As I watch our little sleep
I check her many times
Listen for her breath
More than just the rise
Can't let my senses be fooled
Not again, even if I wake her
I will know she is asleep
And nothing more.
They tell me it was raining
I remember it being wet
But was that from the sky
Or my soul, I wasn't sure yet
The depth of this pain
Cannot be described
Only those who have been here
Tried and failed to make a bribe
I know that I missed it
The moment of your death

I wasn't there to see
You take your last breath.

Grey

Color drains away
Once a masterpiece
Holds no value
Offers no release
A beautiful symphony
With a melody so sweet
I don't hear a note
Not even a beat
It's like without you here
There is nothing worthwhile
I feel like Captain Hook
Chasing after a crocodile
Waiting for the clock to run out
For time to stop or go
Either one, neither one
I am not here nor fro
All I do is sit and wait
For the day to arrive
When we can be together
Instead of just survive
There is no color without you
There is no music or art
There is nothing left
Except for my broken heart.

Today

Today the world is over
There isn't any joy to feel
There isn't a thought to think
And there is no way to heal
I once was surrounded
With so much more than love
I can't find the right words
There's nothing to speak of
Now that you're gone
I can hardly even say it
There is a swirl I can't avoid
I wish I could just quit
But I heard what you said
You are the coat I have to wear
To keep you in her memory
And this I will do, I swear
I look back on all we did
On every moment that we shared
On inside jokes and treats
Everything that showed you cared
It wasn't always rainbows
We had our share of fights
It led to compromise and growth
But still some lonely nights
I can't see a future
Not a thing without you

But I am not alone
And I know I have to.

Roller Coaster

Hold on tight here comes the drop
Ready or not, better grab the side
Inside, my stomach is about to flop
We're on this never-ending ride
Is it the kind that goes way up high
Swinging to and from
Closing your eyes helps
Not a whole lot but some
Or is it the one that spins
Round and round faster still
Better hold my breath
It's about to make me ill
Or the one where the bottom falls
Even when you know it's about—
To go, it still catches you off guard
Leaving me just to shout
Yell and scream or hold it in
There is nothing to be in control of
That is how I feel all the time
Guilt and gravity from above
There is so much pressure to carry
When you carry the weight alone
There is so much that can go wrong
When your heart turns to stone
I want to get off this ride
I don't like this roller coaster

Time and the whole world
Keep moving in a blur
If I sit still and catch my breath
Take just a second for myself
Too bad I can't do that
When you're sitting on a shelf
I'll hold her hand but it's only one
So much that we just can't do
While we wait our turn in line
Waiting there without you
She is too young for this ride
To have to deal with all this now
But death and loss know no age
And they don't care anyhow.

How Could You

If I close my eyes I see you there
You grasp my hand and I know you care
I feel safe, bound in your embrace
What I wouldn't do for just a taste
This is the life that we waited for
These are the moments we had in-store
I don't dare, won't open up my eyes
I can't bear to live without the lies
How could you… I know it's not your fault
How could you… still it makes me halt
How could you… knowing there was a chance
How could you… leave me in this trance
This is how a heart breaks
Giving everything with no one to take
I never thought I could be so strong
But I've been doing it all along
I know that somehow you see
That I am building us, her and me

She knows you and she loves you
What was once three, but now two
Your heart, your light will carry on
And even though it weighs a ton
She will always know who you are
And look up to find your shining star.

Close my Eyes

Close my eyes and hope to hear
In the silence without you there
A notion that you're still around
But nothing will make this seem fair
I can drown out the clang and bang
Of all the people who fawn
At first, they seemed to be here
But no longer are they drawn
Sitting in our little house
Which you turned into a home
Surrounded by our old friends
And yet still I am so alone

I miss the sound of your bike
Revving up and down the road
I miss the thought of plans
All the seeds left unsown
I miss being in the garage
The noise your tools make
One of the many things
Without you I cannot fake
Even in a crowded room
All I hear are my ears ringing
The sound of your silence
Is so much more than deafening.

Reflection

What is it that you see
When you deign to look at me
In your heart or in your head
Or with your eyes instead

Do you see someone weak
Is that why you no longer speak
Or is it that I am now too frail
Somehow lacking in detail

Can you see the darkness in my eye
The pain and fear I hold inside
You say I am so strong
Haven't I been all along

Do you focus on the change
I think that's so strange
I'm trying to keep things the same
Yet what I feel most is shame

Loss is loss but it's not all equal
God, I miss the smell of diesel
Looking for someone to care
All I'm met with is an empty stare

Sometimes I feel like drowning
Reaching out, phone ringing
But no one answers the call
No one sees me at all.

The Life of My Love

Staring up at you
I have no idea what to do
Reality comes knocking, slam
Nothing else is worth a damn
If I have to stay here without you

Into this awful life, I'm thrust
Hold my head high, I know I must
Longing for one more embrace
Yearning to see the smile on your face
How can I be expected to adjust

A mistake, this cannot be correct
You, who is owed so much respect
Our love now lost in drought
Nothing but pain to sprout
In our garden left to neglect

I know you look down from above
I feel you around me like a glove
Almost touching, trying to heal
Pushing me through this ordeal
Even if it feels more like a shove

I still don't know how this can be
That this is the life left for me

Holding strong to your essence
Trying to reach acceptance
To live a life I hope you see.

I Noticed

34

Did you think I didn't notice
When the holiday came and went
And there was no place to go over
How do you think it was spent?

Did you think I didn't notice
On my birthday or even his
That there was no call or plan
No "let me take care of this"

Did you think I didn't notice
That our picture once framed
No longer hangs in the hall
Our spot has been reclaimed

Did you think I didn't notice
Never thought that I might
Hear the words behind my back
Things said in slight

Did you think I didn't notice
How responses got further apart
Almost nonexistent
Like my place in your heart

Did you think I didn't notice
The side-eye that you hid
Let me tell you something:
I did.

As If

As if I hadn't shed long ago
The guilt of expectations so
As if you heard when I've spoken
How I'm past bent and broken
As if I have time to sit and think,
No, but there is the kitchen sink.
As if I had a thought to spare
Here comes the dread and fear.
As if I could say what you wanted to hear
Isn't that what you're looking for
Here comes the request for my time
That looks like a little but isn't mine
Feels like a demand that isn't fair
Across the land, for you to share.
As if I don't have to work all day
Get up and go, dragons to slay
As if I don't have a little to keep
Attention, love—dare not weep
As if sunrise to set isn't well spent
Without a moment left unkept
Here comes your need of me
Because you want to poke in and see
Dissect every word and dispute
Just to say, "That's so cute."
As if I'm not drowning in pressure
This life I can't even measure

As if every second isn't planned for
As if I need another, just one more
Here comes a brick to break inside
Every corner that is mine, can't I hide
Here comes the overexposed
Just to later be disposed.
As if you could handle the storm inside
The thunder booming in my mind
Yes, I am tired, you say I always am
That hurt, what a slam
Here I am drowning in loneliness
Instead of a raft, throw shadiness
You shout, "Oh what fun
Out there swimming in the sun"
As if you saying I'm doing so well
Is just supposed to make me swell
As if every hurdle just crumbles
Because you say I'm humble
As if my life of cards is just illusion
A falsehood, story, collusion
As if I have time for your demands
I have enough in my hands
And speaking of time management
and with whom your day is spent
Let me be the monster who pulls her away
Don't ever tell her that she can't stay
She should feel welcome all the time
And if she's not, that's totally fine
I can keep her at a distance

So here's your song and dance
You asked for a letter
But I'll do you one better.

I am not enough

I never really felt like just being me
Was enough to fill the space
Like something was missing
Something I couldn't place
Always overlooked
Often forgotten and left out
It keeps happening
Inside I can't help but shout
And then I met my love
And he filled that hole
I wasn't alone and it was clear
Together, we were a goal
I can't express the way
Love fills you up, changes
The way you see the world
What's important rearranges
But when that love gets lost
Your heart breaks, future stolen
Everything around you stops
As if the world is frozen
Sitting at home, more alone
Than I have ever been before
Trying to reach out, spend time
Even if it is just to go to the store
Calls go unanswered, plans ignored
My little one cries for her father

Missing him as she should
That knife cuts a little sharper
As I try to tell her it's just me
That Mommy has to be enough
When even I don't feel it
God, I tell you that's rough.

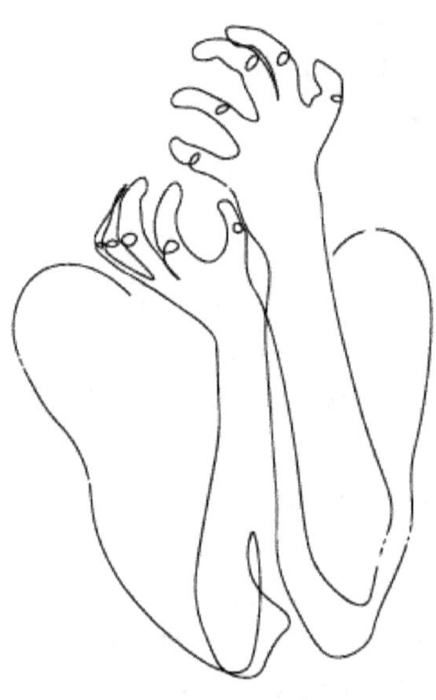

What's That Sound

Here I sit, waiting
Just waiting
Waiting for a call or anything at all
I'm not really the kind to just wait
    tick–
I'm not sure
Not really sure
If this is what I should do
This waiting for you thing
    tick–
Part of me feels
Just a small part
Feels that it's a waste of time
Wasting time, care, all of it
    tick tick–
On you. On me.
On Us.
If there is even a thing to waste
Or wait on, is there?
    creek–
You say there could be
I want it
But I have to wonder
Wonder if you do
    creek, tick–
I'm not sure

Not really sure
If I could take it
If you changed your mind
        creek creek–
I am worth the time
Aren't I?
That we could spend
Together for a while
        crack–
But then I just fill
Get filled with
Hope? Joy?
Fear. Loss. Worry
        crunch–
What if
Just if
I'm not enough?
If no one else thinks so
        break–
Do you know what
What it sounds like
When your heart breaks
Or rips apart?
        rip–
I do.

Ms. Too Independent

When we are little girls
Our moms teach us to be strong
That you don't need a man
Be there, not just tag along
They teach us all the things
The hard way, they found out
Like stashing a bit of money
Be prepared for a reroute.
Life doesn't always go to plan
And when we get a bit older
We enter the world on our own
And more burden we shoulder
We form our circle and build
And start to get by ourselves
Put this independent need away
Store it up on the shelves
One day something changes
A small crack, one fumble
But that grows into more and
What you built starts to crumble
You go it alone, you make do
Find the spot on that bookshelf
Find it, Wake it up, Dust it off
You pull down your inner self
Does there come a time when
When others hold no need?

I can do it myself, I have for so long
I have proven that again indeed
So when life throws a new curve
You won't find me scrambling
Am I now too independent
Is there even such a thing?

I Hear You

I can hear your words
Though I see not your face
I can tell the way it looks
Let me slow down, match your pace
I cannot say what will help
Make you better, no words will
But I can hear your words
I can listen and be still
I understand the pain
I feel your sorrow,
And just because I care
I will call again tomorrow
I can hear your words
And hope I have shown
That someone cares
Even through the phone

How are you today?
Glad to hear it's going well
What can I help you with?
Come on out of that shell
A quick question to start
Now let's dive in deep
Don't be afraid to ask
It's okay to weep
I am here to help

Make it stress-free
Take away the hassle
You can trust me
I hear what you say
Understand what you don't
I can connect the lines
Get to where you want

It's me again,
I hope I'm not annoying
I kind of have to say
That I am a bit enjoying
These moments together
Not much needs to be spoken
But a bit of new life
Perhaps feels awoken
There's a smile
No, don't hide it
Let it shine bright
Be you, and don't quit.

What happens if

These questions in my head
All day long just floating
I try to make them stop
Instead, they keep encroaching
What if something happens to me?
What if she gets hurt?
What if I mess her up?
I scream inside to not blurt
I like to think that I can
To feel capable of raising her
To do this on my own
But then I hear, nevermore
What if she hates me?
What if she leaves?
What if I can't do this?
The answers I can't conceive
I have to make her smile
I have to give her hope
Together we can do this
That's the only way to cope
So then flip my thoughts
And deep down I know
I'll figure this out, I will
So now it's time to show
What if she is amazing?
What if she succeeds?

What if so do I?
That's how we will proceed.

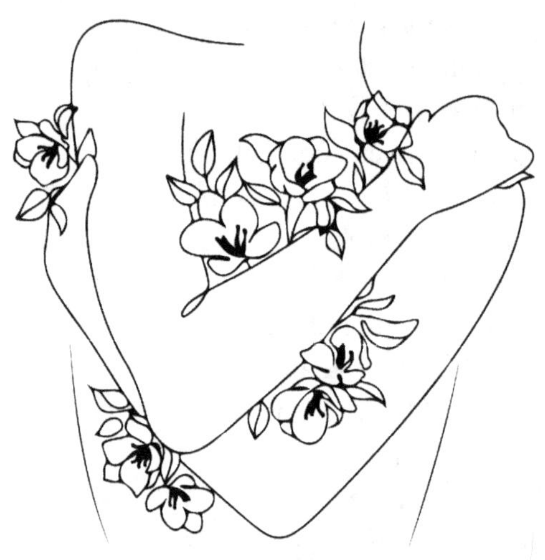

Yesterday

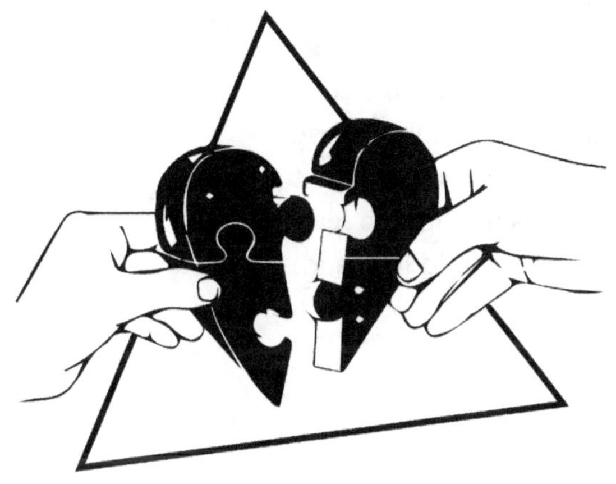

They say time heals all
Well, that's a load of crock
Time teaches you new skills
You don't heal by a clock
With time comes understanding
And still, tasks to do
Responsibilities don't stop
And so, neither can you
Yesterday I was broken
Thought beyond repair
But each day a little more
A little less despair
I move forward, for him
I cannot be stagnant
It is my job to live our future

And carry on his fragment
Every moment that he misses
I must experience twice
In my head I tell myself
This is going to suffice
There is a darkness ahead
Not the future I planned
He holds the light to lead
Until I can hold his hand.

Unspoken

All the things I want to say
But time just slipped away
I thought there would be tomorrow
Now, I'm just left with sorrow
So many words left unspoken
Holding this cheap little token
How could you not see
Everything you meant to me?
It's been far too long
But when I hear our song
I can't help but melt away
There's so much more to say
But no more time for words
I'm sitting here like a coward

Barely moving on with this life
Wondering if I'm still a wife
You meant the world to me
Yet there was something I couldn't see
Was there a darkness in your eye
Was it there for me to find
Something hidden under your surface
No, I don't think that was the case
It happened and you're gone
And now I'm all alone.

I promise

I promise I won't always get it right
And I will probably hold you too tight
And even when you want to run away
You will always have a place to stay
I promise to watch you grow
And mind the seeds that you sow
I may not agree with every choice
But so proud when you use your voice
I'll try to listen to what you say
I promise to keep you safe every day
And your daddy will watch over at night
Just to see your face so bright
And when those thoughts make you cry
I promise to help keep your face dry
My little girl, I would give you it all
Everything, there is no joy too small
There is pain in this world, as you know
And each day can bring a new woe
I promise to help get you through
Even when I don't have a clue
To shine your light into the dark
And help stoke the fire from your spark
I promise to hear with my heart
To watch you like a work of art
To listen with an open mind
And always keep my words kind

I promise we will fight sometimes
A mountain we will have to climb
But there are no roots on the plain
No rainbows without first the rain
I promise to care like a mother should
To protect you like Daddy if he could
To support your every adventure
And to love you with all I am, forever.

A single moment

Today we drove your truck
Just a little trip to the store
Had to grab her some fruit
And honestly nothing more
But while we were there
Of course, she wanted a toy
Because what four-year-old doesn't
And it brings her so much joy
We gathered up our things
Checked out, and left the place
Got your truck all loaded
You should have seen her face
I drive the truck so rarely, see,
Because it reminds me of you
And how it's your truck, not mine
But it must remind her too.
And so this simple thing today
A single moment that we spent
Filled my heart with glee for her
And sadness, heaven sent.

Ohana

Our family is small and broken
We are missing roles and parts
But what we lack in numbers
We make up for in heart
If you look at us and feel sad
I understand why you would
But where most see less
We have more than you could
We fill our missing hole
With more love than ever
We grow together around it
And our bond cannot sever
His memory is always present
His presence stronger
And no one proves that better
Than our beautiful daughter
As I lift her to the sky
I feel his arms around us
He is our guardian angel
In that faith, and him, I trust
Our path is not an easy one
I wish that we weren't on it
But life isn't wishes and rainbows
Sometimes you deal with grit
The hard times in life make us better
Everyday we grow and cope

With one thing or another
But mostly, with hope.

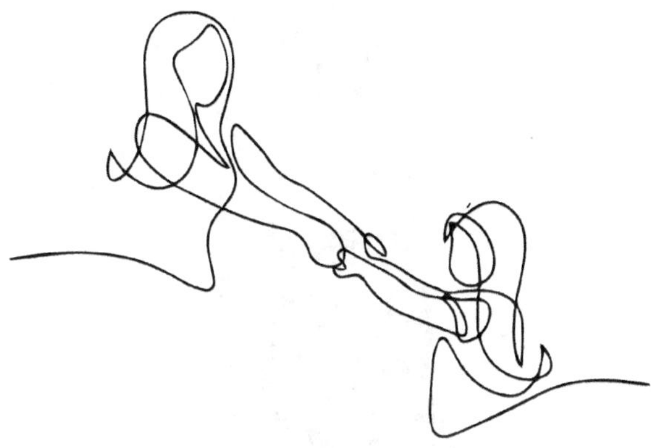

57

Precious Little Girl

Precious little girl
Eyes so full of wonder
All the things I want to say
From the ground 6 feet under
I see you run and play
I hear the way you giggle
Too much umph to go slow
You sit just to wiggle
Please know that I love you
Your name I dare not speak
So many questions must linger
The answers that you seek

Precious little girl
Eyes so full of wonder
All the things I want to say
From the ground 6 feet under
What I wouldn't give to hold you
My last breath long gone
Every night before bed
Know I still sing your song
As you sleep the night away
Tell the monsters not to bite
Or the gremlins, for if they do
They will have a Daddy fight

Precious little girl
Eyes so full of wonder
All the things I want to say
From the ground 6 feet under
This wasn't what we planned
I should have still been there
I hate that I'm stuck here
Please know that I care
There is so much ahead
So many dreams to achieve
So many words left unspoken
I'm sorry I had to leave

Precious little girl
Eyes so full of wonder
All the things I want to say

From the ground 6 feet under
As you grow so big and strong
Each milestone you make
Every memory I miss
My broken heart still aches
Your smile so big and bright
Your heart so full of love
When you feel a wee bit nervous
It's me that gives you a shove

Precious little girl
Eyes so full of wonder
All the things I want to say
From the ground 6 feet under.

www.ingramcontent.com/pod-product-compliance
Lightning Source LLC
LaVergne TN
LVHW021237200726
843509LV00012B/1503